This planner belongs to:

____

Twenty-one

January

S	M	T	W	T	F	S
					1	2
3	4	5	6	7	8	9
10	11	12	13	14	15	16
17	18	19	20	21	22	23
24	25	26	27	28	29	30
31						

February

S	M	T	W	T	F	S
	1	2	3	4	5	6
7	8	9	10	11	12	13
14	15	16	17	18	19	20
21	22	23	24	25	26	27
28						

March

S	M	T	W	T	F	S
	1	2	3	4	5	6
7	8	9	10	11	12	13
14	15	16	17	18	19	20
21	22	23	24	25	26	27
28	29	30	31			

April

S	M	T	W	T	F	S
				1	2	3
4	5	6	7	8	9	10
11	12	13	14	15	16	17
18	19	20	21	22	23	24
25	26	27	28	29	30	

May

S	M	T	W	T	F	S
						1
2	3	4	5	6	7	8
9	10	11	12	13	14	15
16	17	18	19	20	21	22
23	24	25	26	27	28	29
30	31					

June

S	M	T	W	T	F	S
		1	2	3	4	5
6	7	8	9	10	11	12
13	14	15	16	17	18	19
20	21	22	23	24	25	26
27	28	29	30			

July

S	M	T	W	T	F	S
				1	2	3
4	5	6	7	8	9	10
11	12	13	14	15	16	17
18	19	20	21	22	23	24
25	26	27	28	29	30	31

August

S	M	T	W	T	F	S
1	2	3	4	5	6	7
8	9	10	11	12	13	14
15	16	17	18	19	20	21
22	23	24	25	26	27	28
29	30	31				

September

S	M	T	W	T	F	S
			1	2	3	4
5	6	7	8	9	10	11
12	13	14	15	16	17	18
19	20	21	22	23	24	25
26	27	28	29	30		

October

S	M	T	W	T	F	S
					1	2
3	4	5	6	7	8	9
10	11	12	13	14	15	16
17	18	19	20	21	22	23
24	25	26	27	28	29	30
31						

November

S	M	T	W	T	F	S
	1	2	3	4	5	6
7	8	9	10	11	12	13
14	15	16	17	18	19	20
21	22	23	24	25	26	27
28	29	30				

December

S	M	T	W	T	F	S
			1	2	3	4
5	6	7	8	9	10	11
12	13	14	15	16	17	18
19	20	21	22	23	24	25
26	27	28	29	30	31	

Year in Pixels

	J	F	M	A	M	J	J	A	S	O	N	D
1.												
2.												
3.												
4.												
5.												
6.												
7.												
8.												
9.												
10.												
11.												
12.												
13.												
14.												
15.												
16.												
17.												
18.												
19.												
20.												
21.												
22.												
23.												
24.												
25.												
26.												
27.												
28.												
29.												
30.												
31.												

Color Codes

Notes

January 2021

SUNDAY	MONDAY	TUESDAY	WEDNESDAY
3	4	5	6
10	11	12	13
17	18	19	20
24	25	26	27

January 2021

THURSDAY	FRIDAY	SATURDAY	NOTES
	1	2	○
			○
			○
			○
			○
7	8	9	○
			○
			○
			○
14	15	16	○
			○
			○
			○
			○
21	22	23	○
			○
			○
			○
			○
28	29	30	31

February 2021

SUNDAY	MONDAY	TUESDAY	WEDNESDAY
	1	2	3
7	8	9	10
14	15	16	17
21	22	23	24
28			

February 2021

THURSDAY	FRIDAY	SATURDAY	NOTES
4	5	6	○
			○
			○
			○
			○
11	12	13	○
			○
			○
			○
18	19	20	○
			○
			○
			○
			○
25	26	27	○
			○
			○
			○
			○
			NOTES

March 2021

SUNDAY	MONDAY	TUESDAY	WEDNESDAY
	1	2	3
7	8	9	10
14	15	16	17
21	22	23	24
28	29	30	31

March 2021

THURSDAY	FRIDAY	SATURDAY	NOTES
4	5	6	○
			○
			○
			○
			○
11	12	13	○
			○
			○
			○
18	19	20	○
			○
			○
			○
25	26	27	○
			○
			○
			○
			○
			NOTES

April 2021

SUNDAY	MONDAY	TUESDAY	WEDNESDAY
4	5	6	7
11	12	13	14
18	19	20	21
25	26	27	28

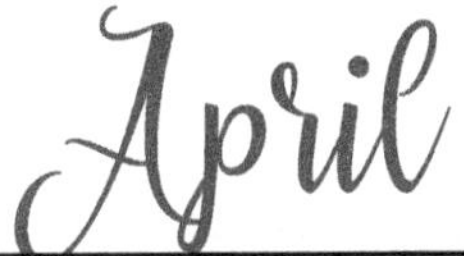

April 2021

THURSDAY	FRIDAY	SATURDAY	NOTES
1	2	3	○
			○
			○
			○
			○
8	9	10	○
			○
			○
			○
15	16	17	○
			○
			○
			○
			○
22	23	24	○
			○
			○
			○
			○
29	30	1	NOTES

May 2021

SUNDAY	MONDAY	TUESDAY	WEDNESDAY
2	3	4	5
9	10	11	12
16	17	18	19
23	24	25	26
30	31		

May 2021

THURSDAY	FRIDAY	SATURDAY	NOTES
6	7	8	○
			○
			○
			○
			○
13	14	15	○
			○
			○
			○
20	21	22	○
			○
			○
			○
			○
27	28	29	○
			○
			○
			○
			○
			NOTES

June 2021

SUNDAY	MONDAY	TUESDAY	WEDNESDAY
		1	2
6	7	8	9
13	14	15	16
20	21	22	23
27	28	29	30

June 2021

THURSDAY	FRIDAY	SATURDAY	NOTES
3	4	5	○
			○
			○
			○
			○
10	11	12	○
			○
			○
			○
17	18	19	○
			○
			○
			○
			○
24	25	26	○
			○
			○
			○
			○
			NOTES

July 2021

SUNDAY	MONDAY	TUESDAY	WEDNESDAY
4	5	6	7
11	12	13	14
18	19	20	21
25	26	27	28

July 2021

THURSDAY	FRIDAY	SATURDAY	NOTES
1	2	3	○
			○
			○
			○
			○
8	9	10	○
			○
			○
			○
15	16	17	○
			○
			○
			○
			○
22	23	24	○
			○
			○
			○
			○
29	30	31	NOTES

August 2021

SUNDAY	MONDAY	TUESDAY	WEDNESDAY
1	2	3	4
8	9	10	11
15	16	17	18
22	23	24	25
29	30	31	

August 2021

THURSDAY	FRIDAY	SATURDAY	NOTES
5	6	7	○
			○
			○
			○
			○
12	13	14	○
			○
			○
			○
19	20	21	○
			○
			○
			○
			○
26	27	28	NOTES

September 2021

SUNDAY	MONDAY	TUESDAY	WEDNESDAY
			1
5	6	7	8
12	13	14	15
19	20	21	22
26	27	28	29

September 2021

THURSDAY	FRIDAY	SATURDAY	NOTES
2	3	4	○
			○
			○
			○
			○
9	10	11	○
			○
			○
			○
16	17	18	○
			○
			○
			○
23	24	25	○
			○
			○
			○
			○
30			NOTES

October 2021

SUNDAY	MONDAY	TUESDAY	WEDNESDAY
3	4	5	6
10	11	12	13
17	18	19	20
24	25	26	27

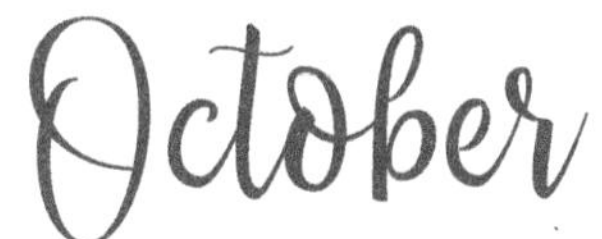

October

2021

THURSDAY	FRIDAY	SATURDAY	NOTES
	1	2	○
			○
			○
			○
			○
7	8	9	○
			○
			○
			○
14	15	16	○
			○
			○
			○
			○
21	22	23	○
			○
			○
			○
			○
28	29	30 / 31 SUNDAY	NOTES

November 2021

SUNDAY	MONDAY	TUESDAY	WEDNESDAY
	1	2	3
7	8	9	10
14	15	16	17
21	22	23	24
28	29	30	

November 2021

THURSDAY	FRIDAY	SATURDAY	NOTES
4	5	6	○
			○
			○
			○
			○
11	12	13	○
			○
			○
			○
18	19	20	○
			○
			○
			○
			○
25	26	27	○
			○
			○
			○
			○
			NOTES

December 2021

SUNDAY	MONDAY	TUESDAY	WEDNESDAY
			1
5	6	7	8
12	13	14	15
19	20	21	22
26	27	28	29

December 2021

THURSDAY	FRIDAY	SATURDAY	NOTES
2	3	4	○
			○
			○
			○
			○
9	10	11	○
			○
			○
			○
			○
16	17	18	○
			○
			○
			○
			○
23	24	25	○
			○
			○
			○
			○
30	31		NOTES

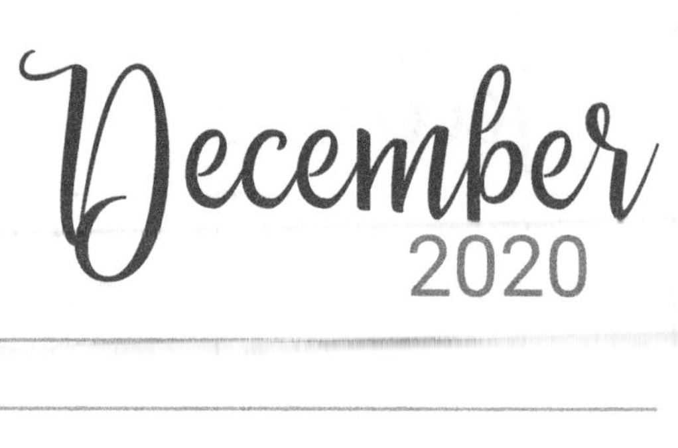

01 TUESDAY

02 WEDNESDAY

03 THURSDAY

04 FRIDAY

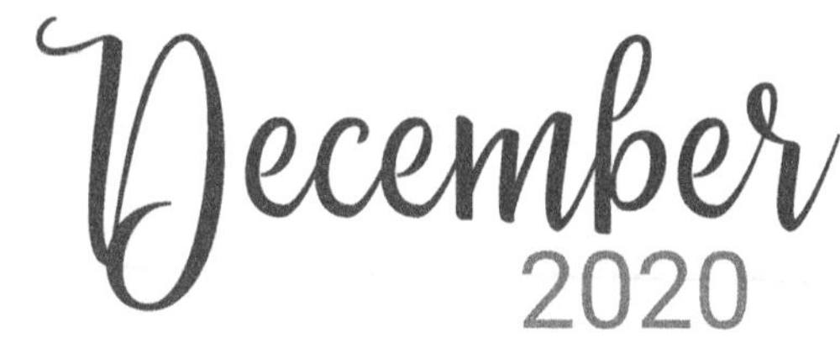

05 SATURDAY

06 SUNDAY

07 MONDAY

08 TUESDAY

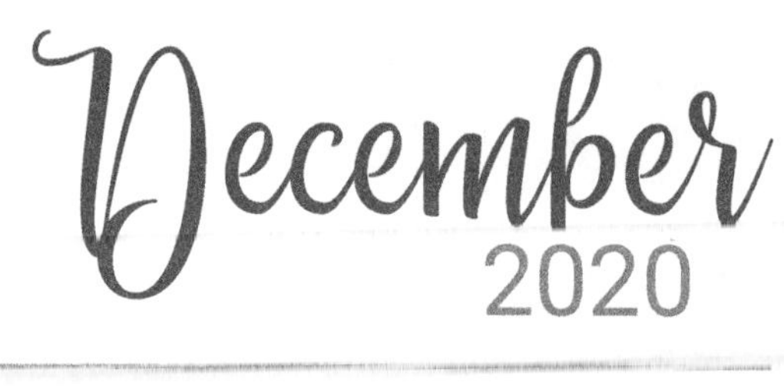

09 WEDNESDAY

10 THURSDAY

11 FRIDAY

12 SATURDAY

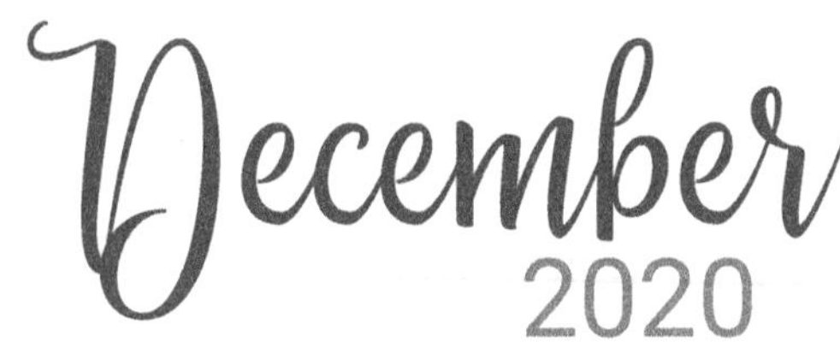

13 SUNDAY

14 MONDAY

15 TUESDAY

16 WEDNESDAY

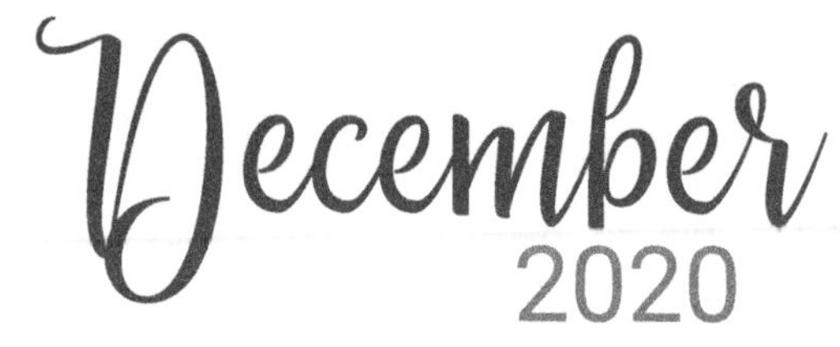

17 THURSDAY

18 FRIDAY

19 SATURDAY

20 SUNDAY

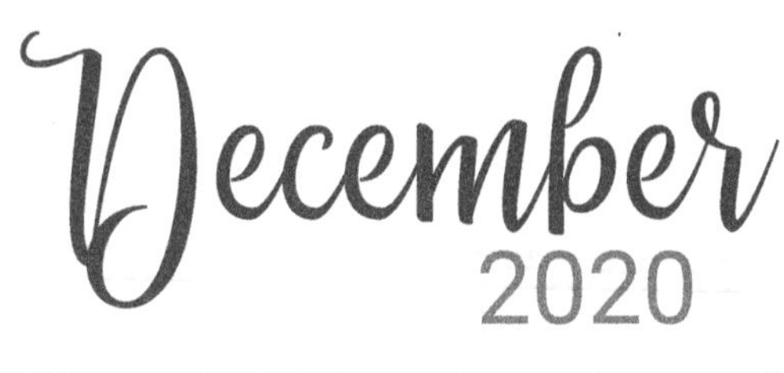

21 MONDAY

22 TUESDAY

23 WEDNESDAY

24 THURSDAY

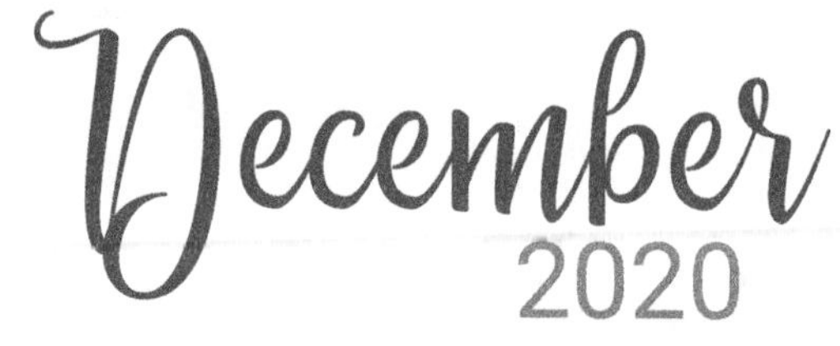

25 FRIDAY

26 SATURDAY

27 SUNDAY

28 MONDAY

December
2020

29 TUESDAY

30 WEDNESDAY

31 THURSDAY

NOTES

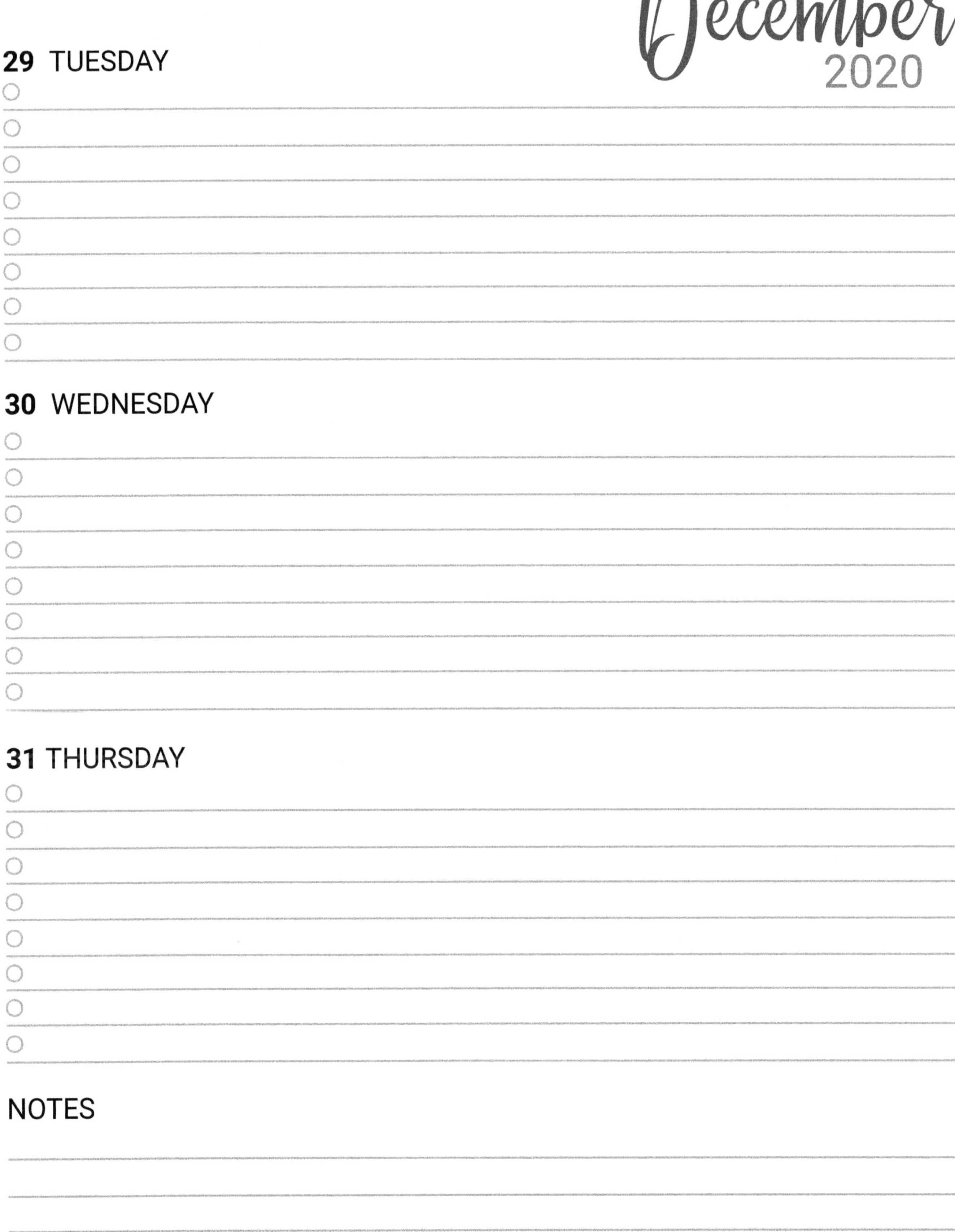

01 FRIDAY

02 SATURDAY

03 SUNDAY

04 MONDAY

January
2021

05 TUESDAY

-
-
-
-
-
-
-
-

06 WEDNESDAY

-
-
-
-
-
-
-
-

07 THURSDAY

-
-
-
-
-
-
-
-

08 FRIDAY

-
-
-
-
-

09 SATURDAY

10 SUNDAY

11 MONDAY

12 TUESDAY

13 WEDNESDAY

14 THURSDAY

15 FRIDAY

16 SATURDAY

17 SUNDAY

18 MONDAY

19 TUESDAY

20 WEDNESDAY

21 THURSDAY

22 FRIDAY

23 SATURDAY

24 SUNDAY

25 MONDAY

26 TUESDAY

27 WEDNESDAY

28 THURSDAY

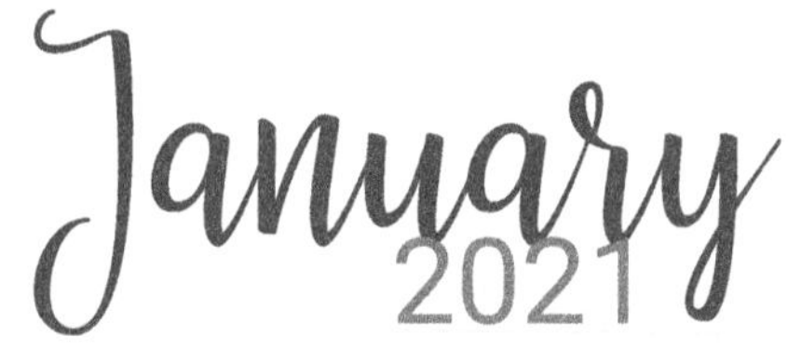

29 FRIDAY

30 SATURDAY

31 SUNDAY

NOTES

February 2021

01 MONDAY

○
○
○
○
○
○
○
○

02 TUESDAY

○
○
○
○
○
○
○
○

03 WEDNESDAY

○
○
○
○
○
○
○
○

04 THURSDAY

○
○
○
○
○

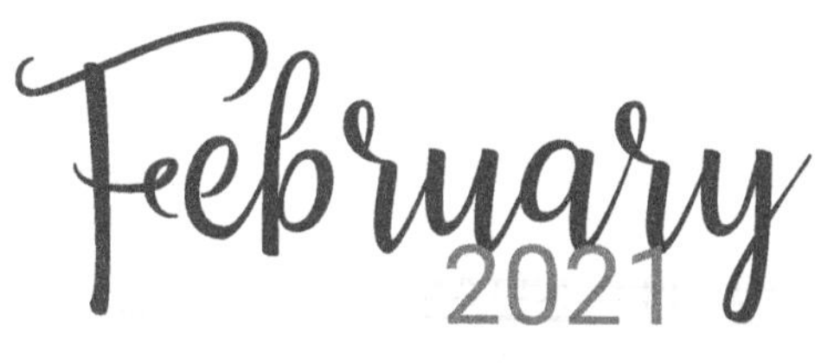

05 FRIDAY

06 SATURDAY

07 SUNDAY

08 MONDAY

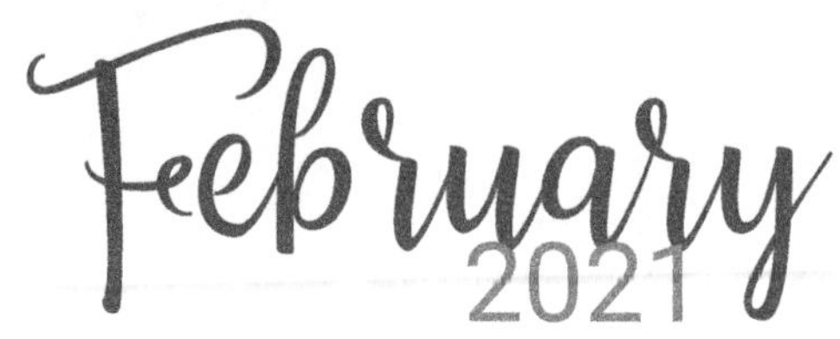

09 TUESDAY

10 WEDNESDAY

11 THURSDAY

12 FRIDAY

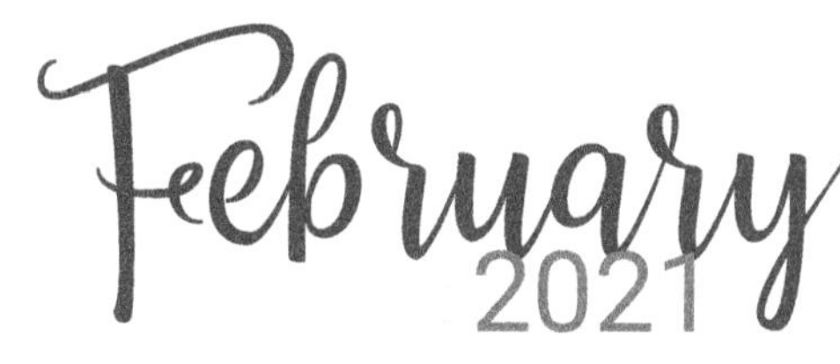

February 2021

13 SATURDAY

14 SUNDAY

15 MONDAY

16 TUESDAY

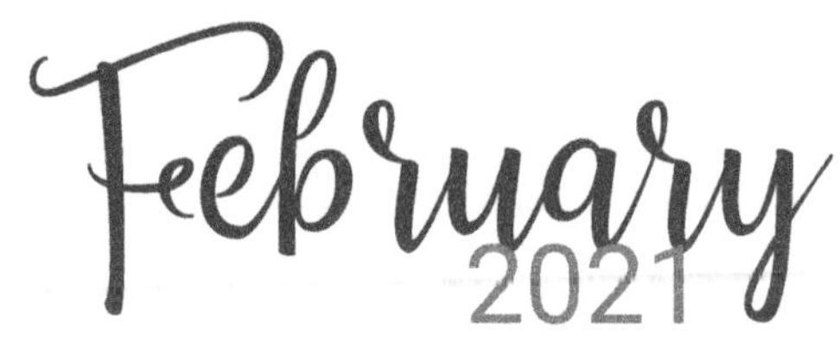

February 2021

17 WEDNESDAY

18 THURSDAY

19 FRIDAY

20 SATURDAY

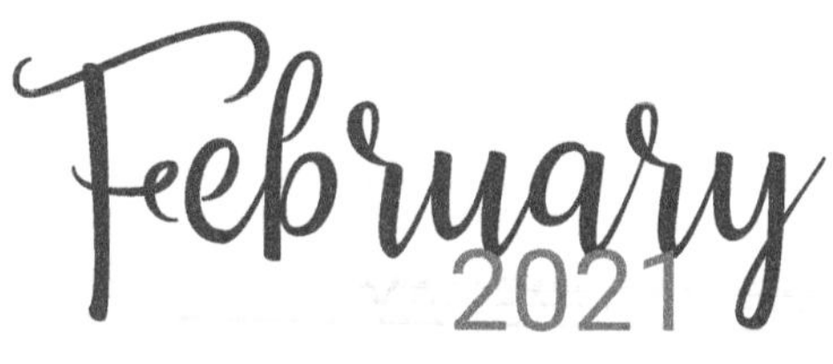

21 SUNDAY

22 MONDAY

23 TUESDAY

24 WEDNESDAY

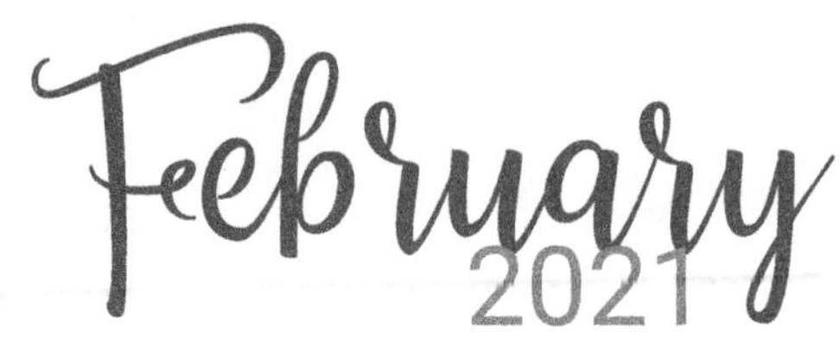

25 THURSDAY

26 FRIDAY

27 SATURDAY

28 SUNDAY

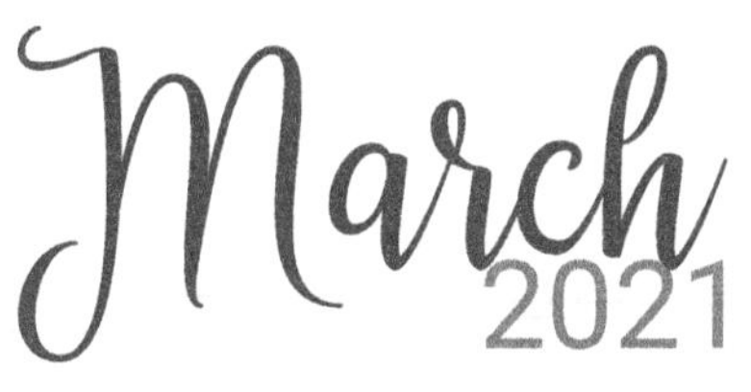

01 MONDAY

02 TUESDAY

03 WEDNESDAY

04 THURSDAY

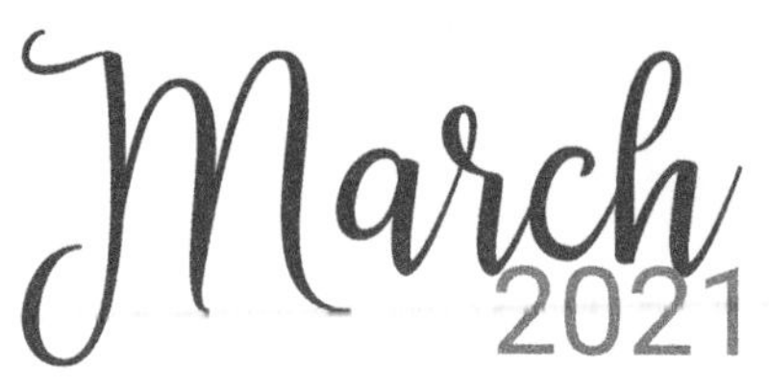

05 FRIDAY

06 SATURDAY

07 SUNDAY

08 MONDAY

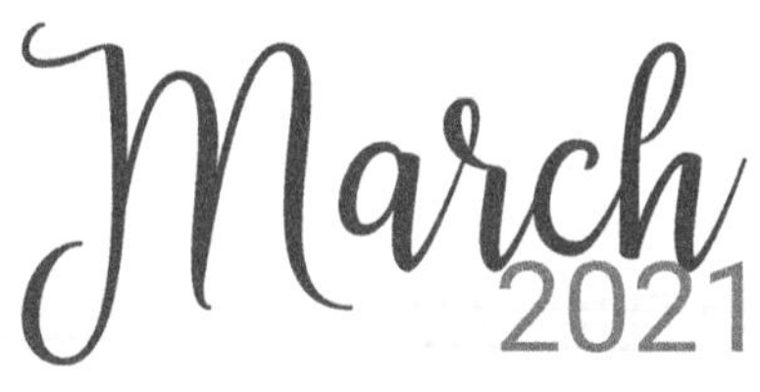

March 2021

09 TUESDAY

10 WEDNESDAY

11 THURSDAY

12 FRIDAY

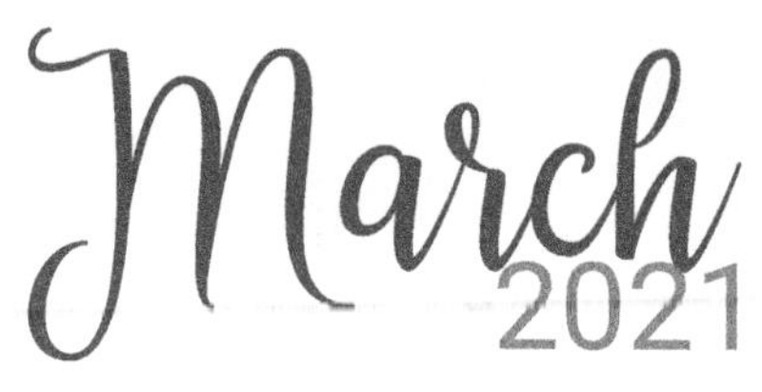

13 SATURDAY

14 SUNDAY

15 MONDAY

16 TUESDAY

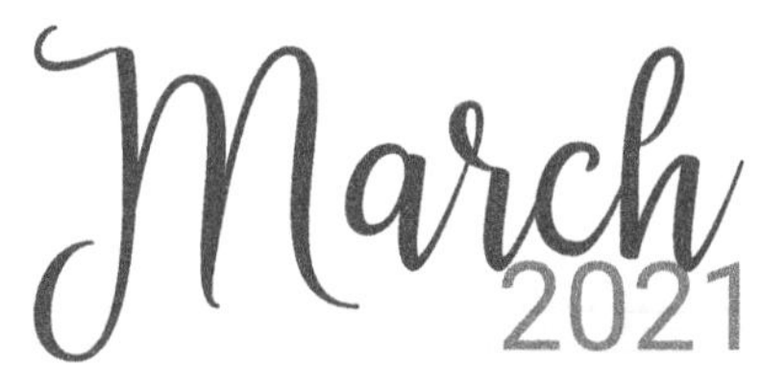

17 WEDNESDAY

18 THURSDAY

19 FRIDAY

20 SATURDAY

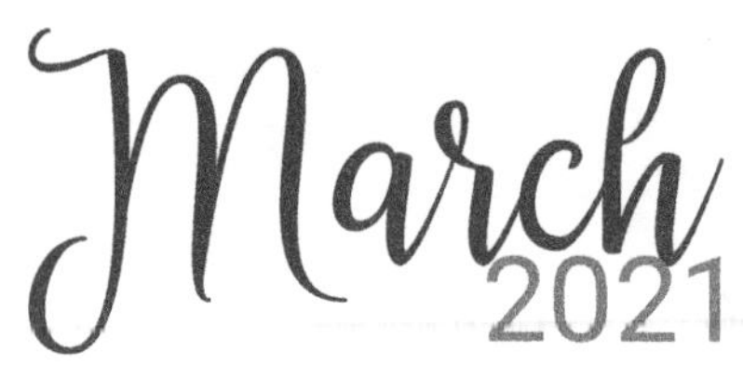

21 SUNDAY

22 MONDAY

23 TUESDAY

24 WEDNESDAY

25 THURSDAY

26 FRIDAY

27 SATURDAY

28 SUNDAY

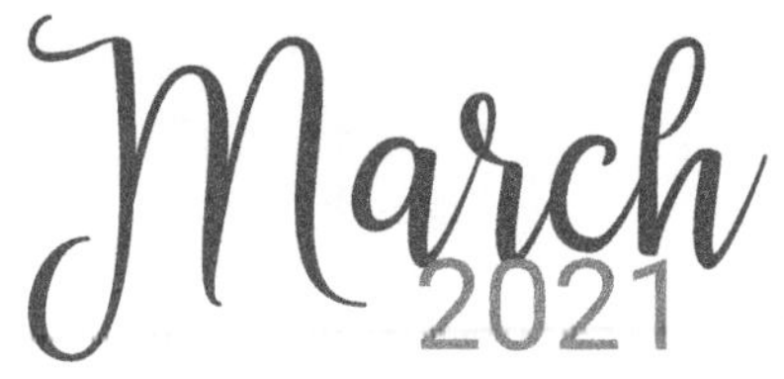

29 MONDAY

○
○
○
○
○
○
○
○

30 TUESDAY

○
○
○
○
○
○
○
○

31 WEDNESDAY

○
○
○
○
○
○
○
○

NOTES

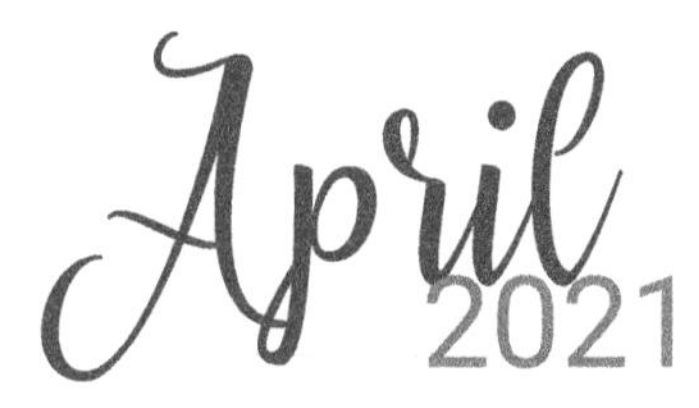

01 THURSDAY

02 FRIDAY

03 SATURDAY

04 SUNDAY

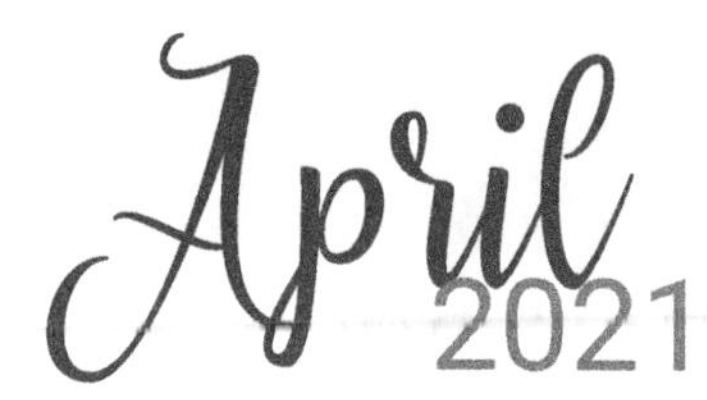

05 MONDAY

06 TUESDAY

07 WEDNESDAY

08 THURSDAY

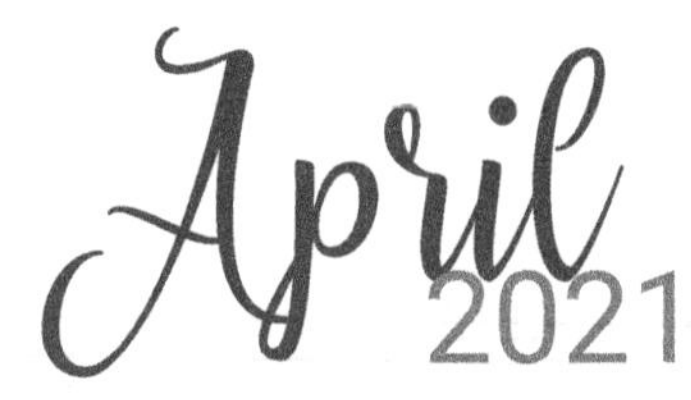

09 FRIDAY

10 SATURDAY

11 SUNDAY

12 MONDAY

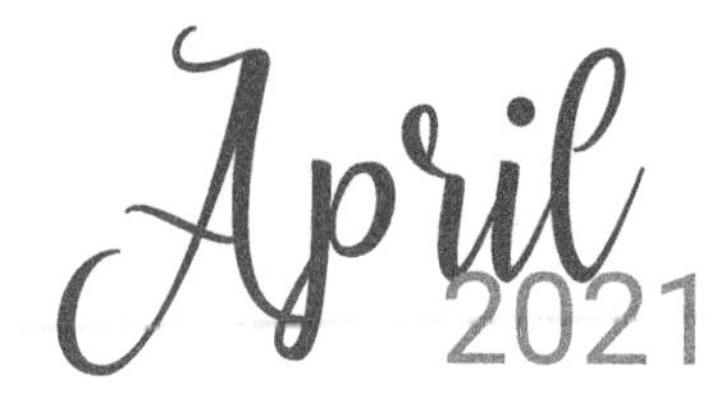

13 TUESDAY

14 WEDNESDAY

15 THURSDAY

16 FRIDAY

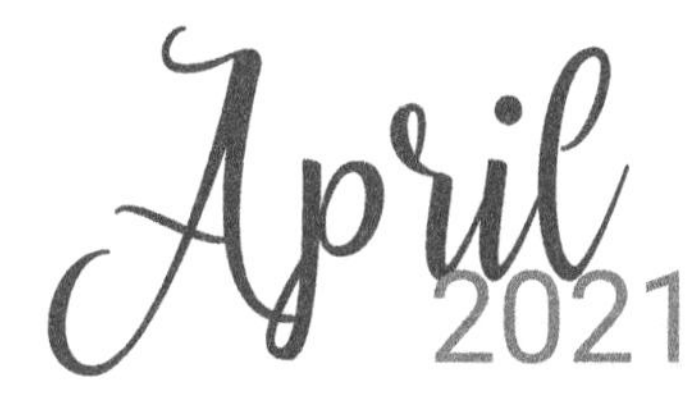

April
2021

17 SATURDAY

18 SUNDAY

19 MONDAY

20 TUESDAY

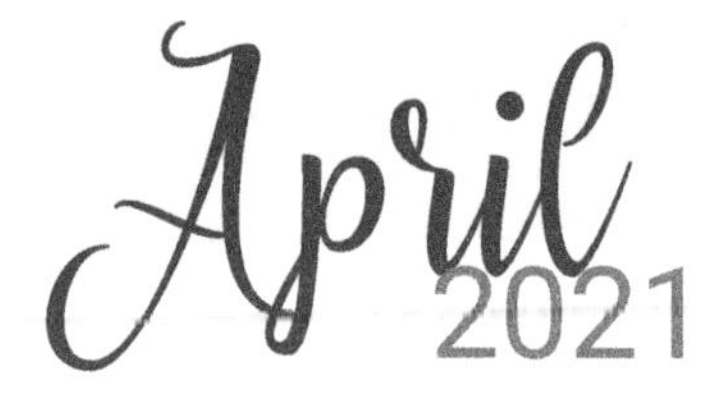

21 WEDNESDAY

22 THURSDAY

23 FRIDAY

24 SATURDAY

April
2021

25 SUNDAY

26 MONDAY

27 TUESDAY

28 WEDNESDAY

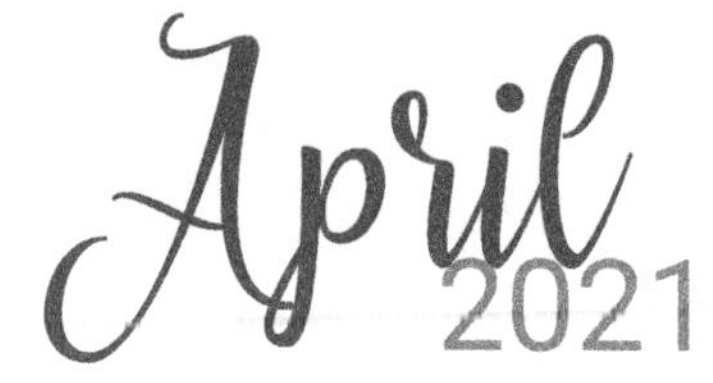

April
2021

29 THURSDAY

30 FRIDAY

NOTES

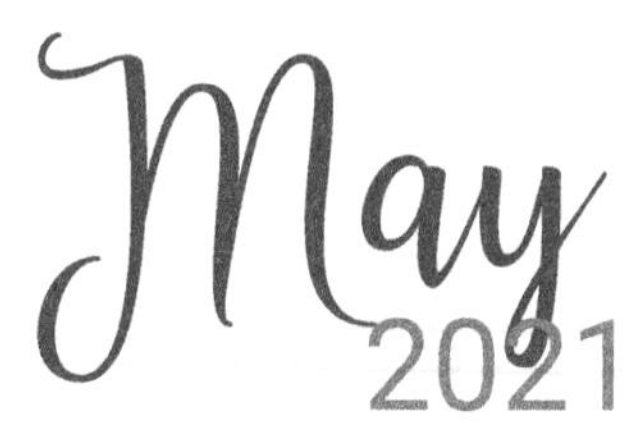

01 SATURDAY

02 SUNDAY

03 MONDAY

04 TUESDAY

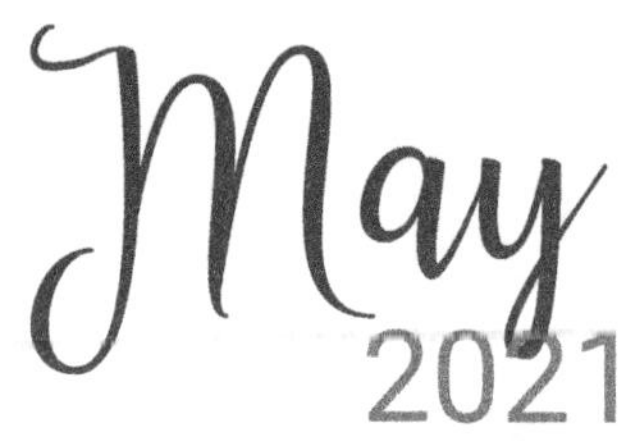

05 WEDNESDAY

06 THURSDAY

07 FRIDAY

08 SATURDAY

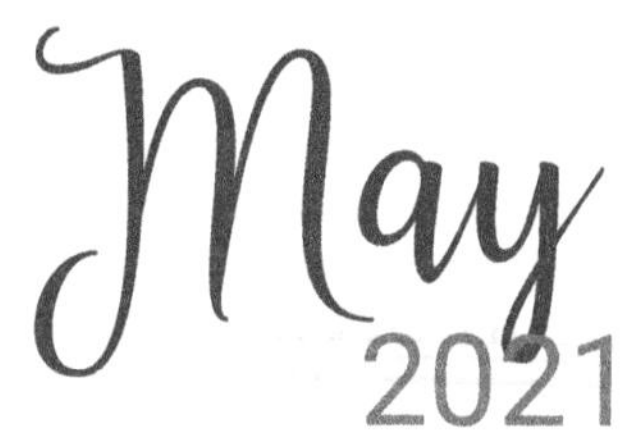

09 SUNDAY

10 MONDAY

11 TUESDAY

12 WEDNESDAY

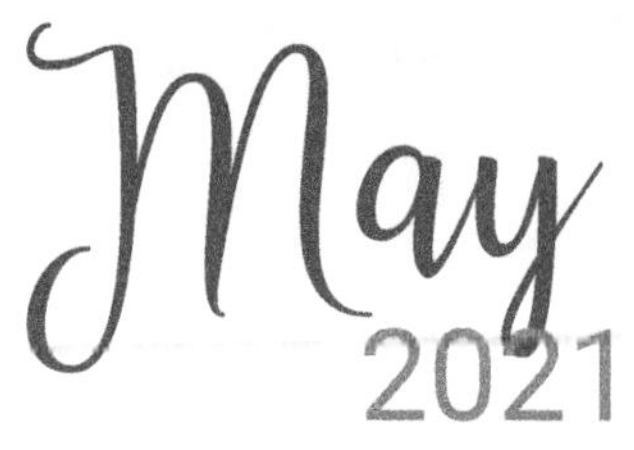

13 THURSDAY

14 FRIDAY

15 SATURDAY

16 SUNDAY

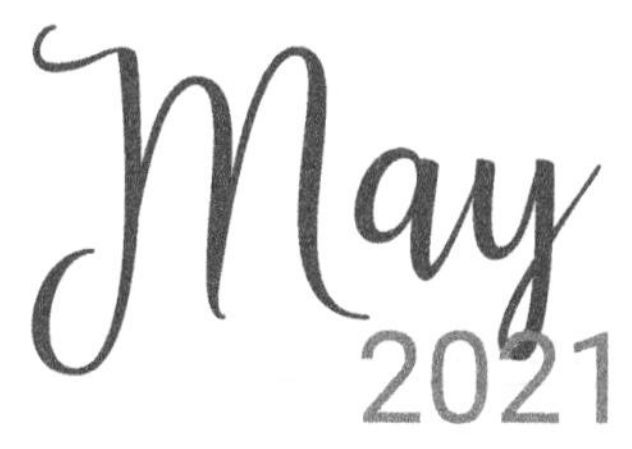

17 MONDAY

18 TUESDAY

19 WEDNESDAY

20 THURSDAY

May 2021

21 FRIDAY

22 SATURDAY

23 SUNDAY

24 MONDAY

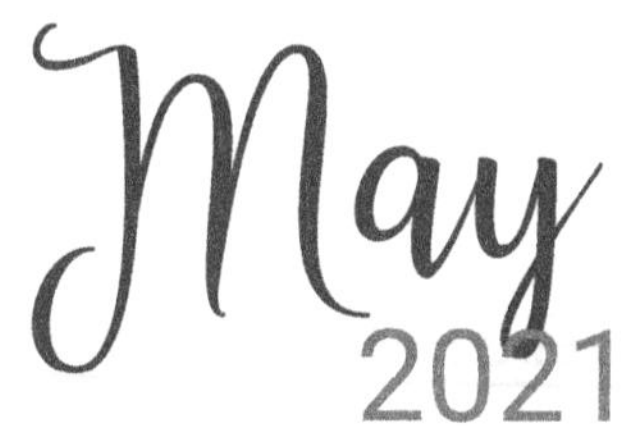

25 TUESDAY

26 WEDNESDAY

27 THURSDAY

28 FRIDAY

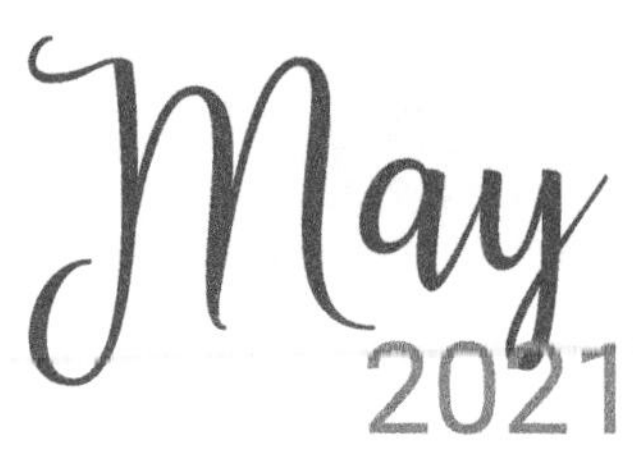

May
2021

29 SATURDAY

30 SUNDAY

31 MONDAY

NOTES

01 TUESDAY

02 WEDNESDAY

03 THURSDAY

04 FRIDAY

June
2021

05 SATURDAY

06 SUNDAY

07 MONDAY

08 TUESDAY

09 WEDNESDAY

10 THURSDAY

11 FRIDAY

12 SATURDAY

June
2021

13 SUNDAY

14 MONDAY

15 TUESDAY

16 WEDNESDAY

17 THURSDAY

18 FRIDAY

19 SATURDAY

20 SUNDAY

21 MONDAY

22 TUESDAY

23 WEDNESDAY

24 THURSDAY

25 FRIDAY

26 SATURDAY

27 SUNDAY

28 MONDAY

29 TUESDAY

- ○
- ○
- ○
- ○
- ○
- ○
- ○
- ○

30 WEDNESDAY

- ○
- ○
- ○
- ○
- ○
- ○
- ○
- ○

NOTES

July
2021

01 THURSDAY

02 FRIDAY

03 SATURDAY

04 SUNDAY

05 MONDAY

○
○
○
○
○
○
○
○

06 TUESDAY

○
○
○
○
○
○
○
○

07 WEDNESDAY

○
○
○
○
○
○
○
○

08 THURSDAY

○
○
○
○
○

09 FRIDAY

10 SATURDAY

11 SUNDAY

12 MONDAY

13 TUESDAY

14 WEDNESDAY

15 THURSDAY

16 FRIDAY

17 SATURDAY

18 SUNDAY

19 MONDAY

20 TUESDAY

21 WEDNESDAY

22 THURSDAY

23 FRIDAY

24 SATURDAY

July
2021

25 SUNDAY

○ ____
○ ____
○ ____
○ ____
○ ____
○ ____
○ ____
○ ____

26 MONDAY

○ ____
○ ____
○ ____
○ ____
○ ____
○ ____
○ ____
○ ____

27 TUESDAY

○ ____
○ ____
○ ____
○ ____
○ ____
○ ____
○ ____
○ ____

28 WEDNESDAY

○ ____
○ ____
○ ____
○ ____
○ ____

29 THURSDAY

30 FRIDAY

31 SATURDAY

NOTES

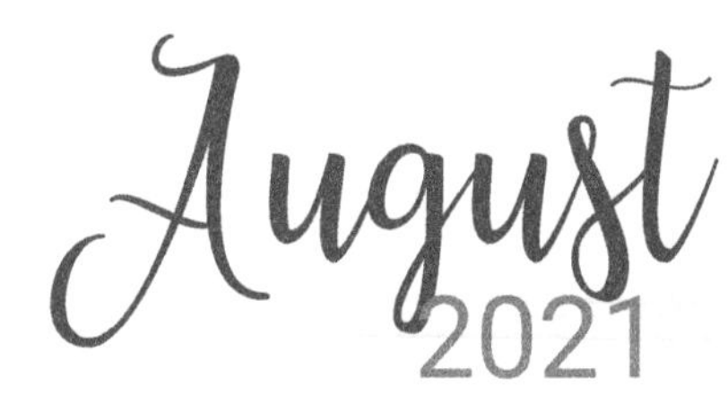

01 SUNDAY

02 MONDAY

03 TUESDAY

04 WEDNESDAY

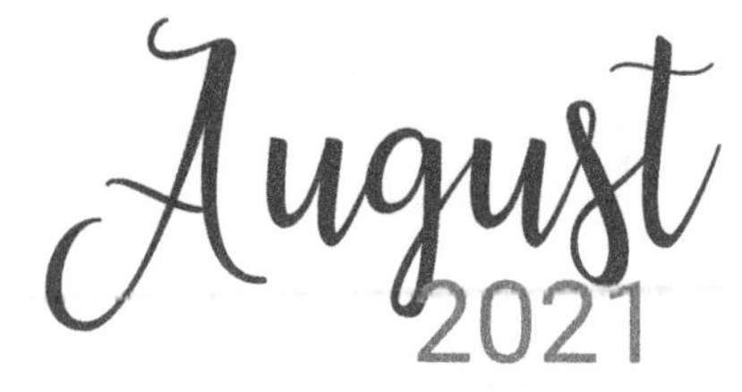

05 THURSDAY

○
○
○
○
○
○
○

06 FRIDAY

○
○
○
○
○
○
○

07 SATURDAY

○
○
○
○
○
○
○
○

08 SUNDAY

○
○
○
○
○

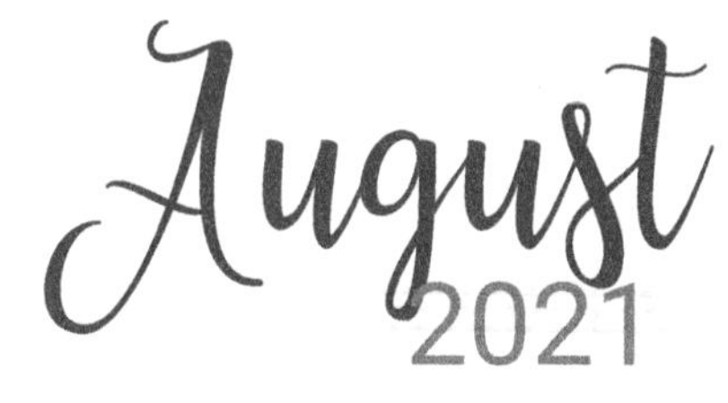

August
2021

09 MONDAY

○ _______________
○ _______________
○ _______________
○ _______________
○ _______________
○ _______________
○ _______________
○ _______________

10 TUESDAY

○ _______________
○ _______________
○ _______________
○ _______________
○ _______________
○ _______________
○ _______________
○ _______________

11 WEDNESDAY

○ _______________
○ _______________
○ _______________
○ _______________
○ _______________
○ _______________
○ _______________
○ _______________

12 THURSDAY

○ _______________
○ _______________
○ _______________
○ _______________
○ _______________

13 FRIDAY

14 SATURDAY

15 SUNDAY

16 MONDAY

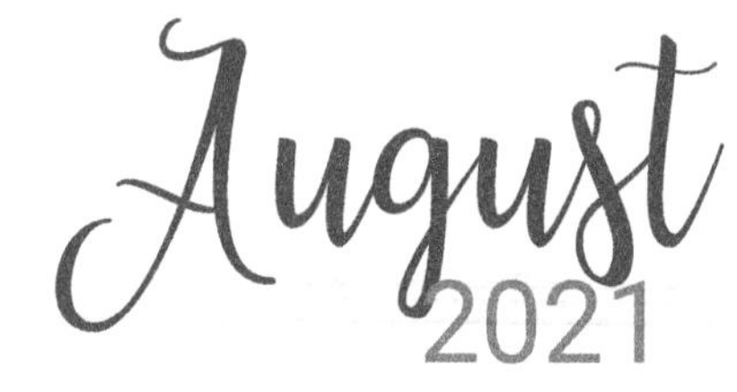

17 TUESDAY

18 WEDNESDAY

19 THURSDAY

20 FRIDAY

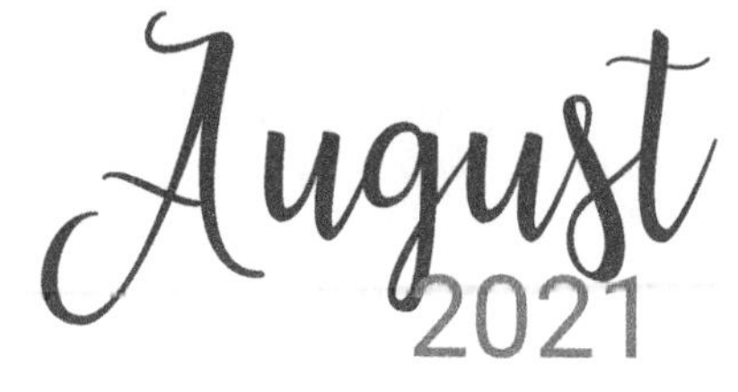

21 SATURDAY

22 SUNDAY

23 MONDAY

24 TUESDAY

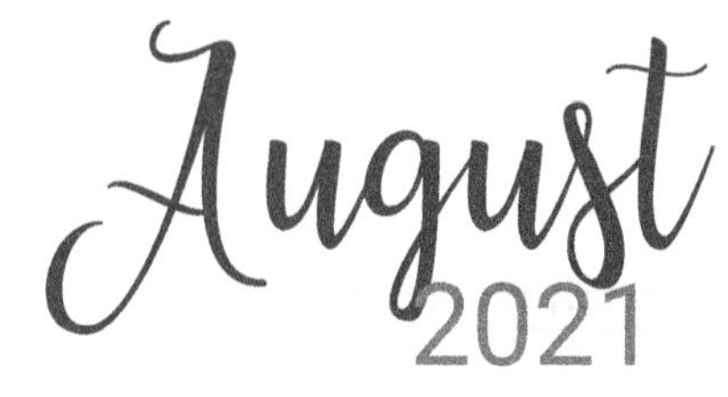

25 WEDNESDAY

26 THURSDAY

27 FRIDAY

28 SATURDAY

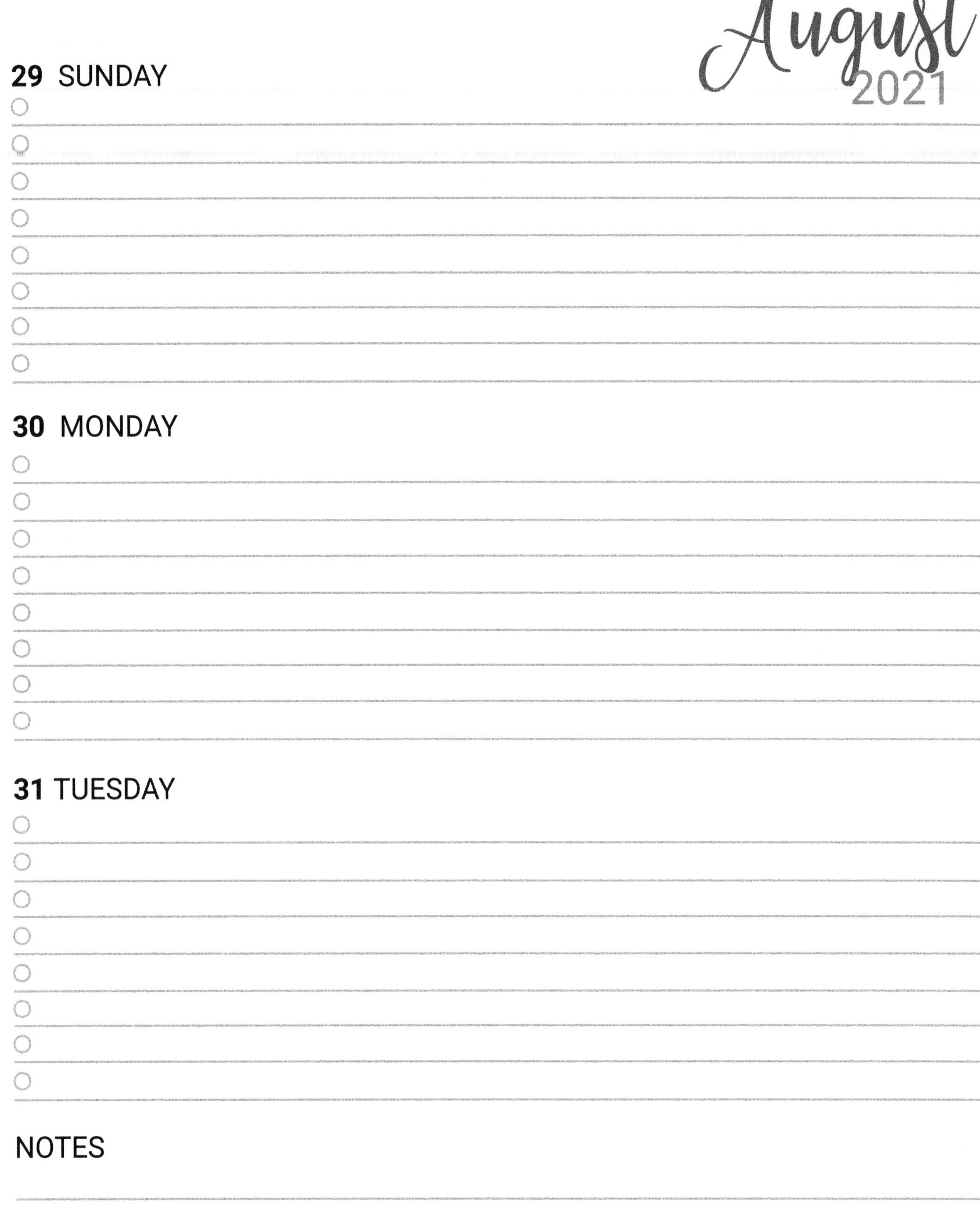

August
2021

29 SUNDAY

30 MONDAY

31 TUESDAY

NOTES

01 WEDNESDAY

02 THURSDAY

03 FRIDAY

04 SATURDAY

05 SUNDAY

06 MONDAY

07 TUESDAY

08 WEDNESDAY

09 THURSDAY

10 FRIDAY

11 SATURDAY

12 SUNDAY

13 MONDAY

14 TUESDAY

15 WEDNESDAY

16 THURSDAY

17 FRIDAY

18 SATURDAY

19 SUNDAY

20 MONDAY

21 TUESDAY

○
○
○
○
○
○
○
○

22 WEDNESDAY

○
○
○
○
○
○
○
○

23 THURSDAY

○
○
○
○
○
○
○
○

24 FRIDAY

○
○
○
○
○

September
2021

25 SATURDAY

26 SUNDAY

27 MONDAY

28 TUESDAY

29 WEDNESDAY

30 THURSDAY

NOTES

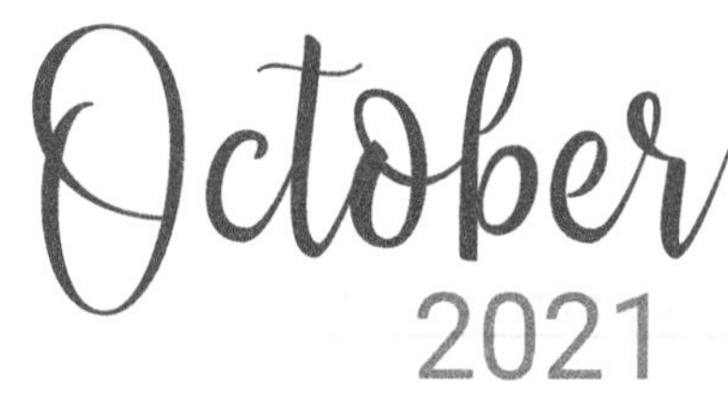

October
2021

01 FRIDAY

02 SATURDAY

03 SUNDAY

04 MONDAY

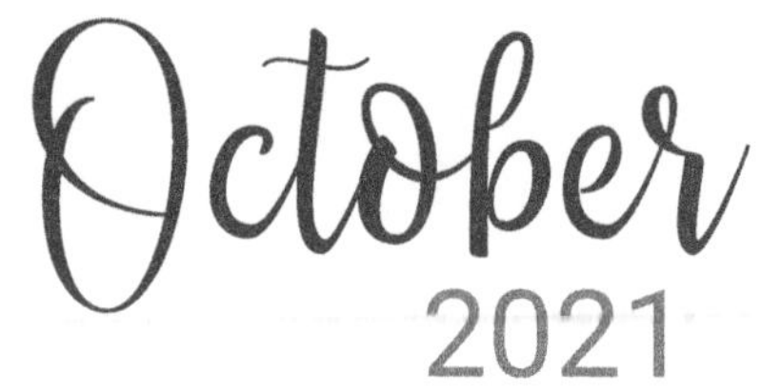

October
2021

05 TUESDAY

06 WEDNESDAY

07 THURSDAY

08 FRIDAY

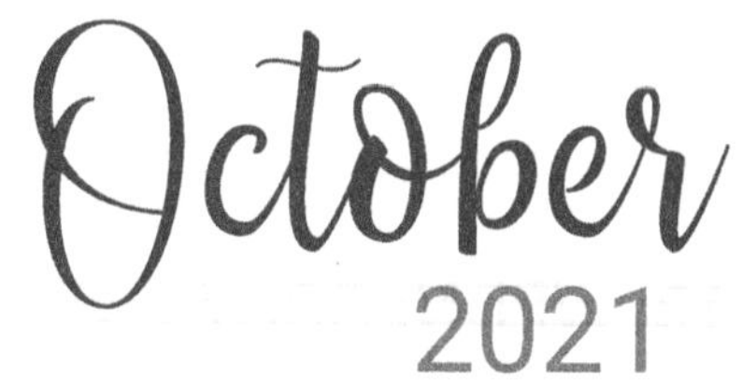

October
2021

09 SATURDAY

10 SUNDAY

11 MONDAY

12 TUESDAY

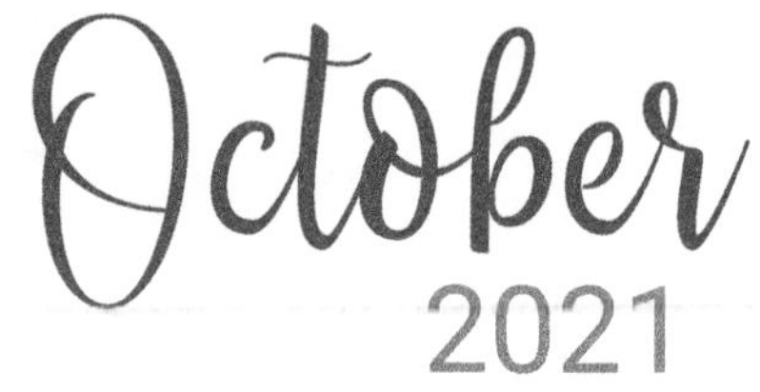

13 WEDNESDAY

14 THURSDAY

15 FRIDAY

16 SATURDAY

October
2021

17 SUNDAY

18 MONDAY

19 TUESDAY

20 WEDNESDAY

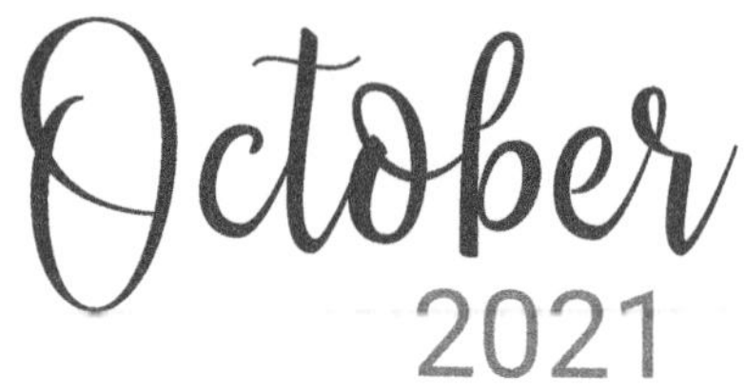

21 THURSDAY

22 FRIDAY

23 SATURDAY

24 SUNDAY

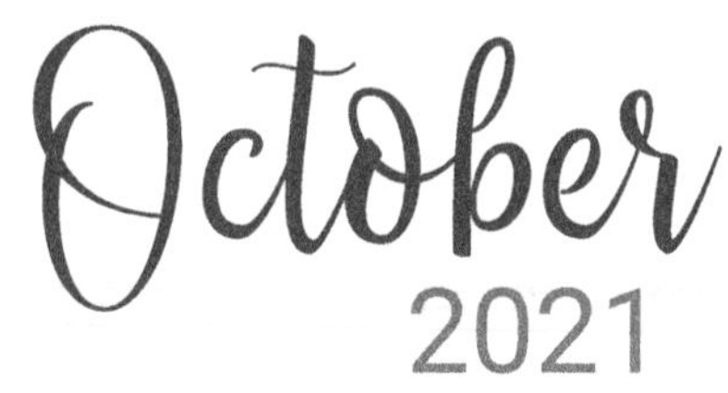

25 MONDAY

26 TUESDAY

27 WEDNESDAY

28 THURSDAY

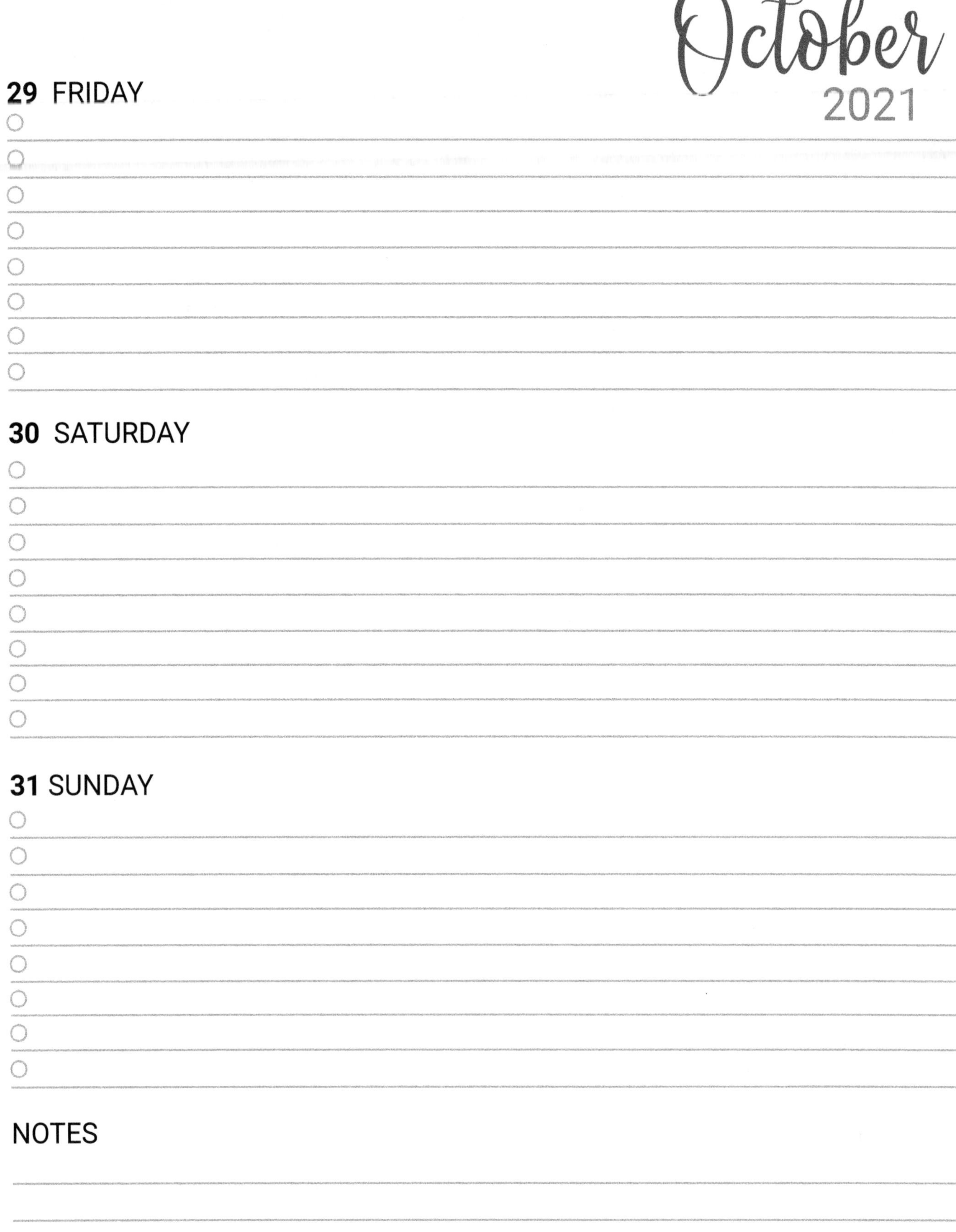

29 FRIDAY

30 SATURDAY

31 SUNDAY

NOTES

01 MONDAY

02 TUESDAY

03 WEDNESDAY

04 THURSDAY

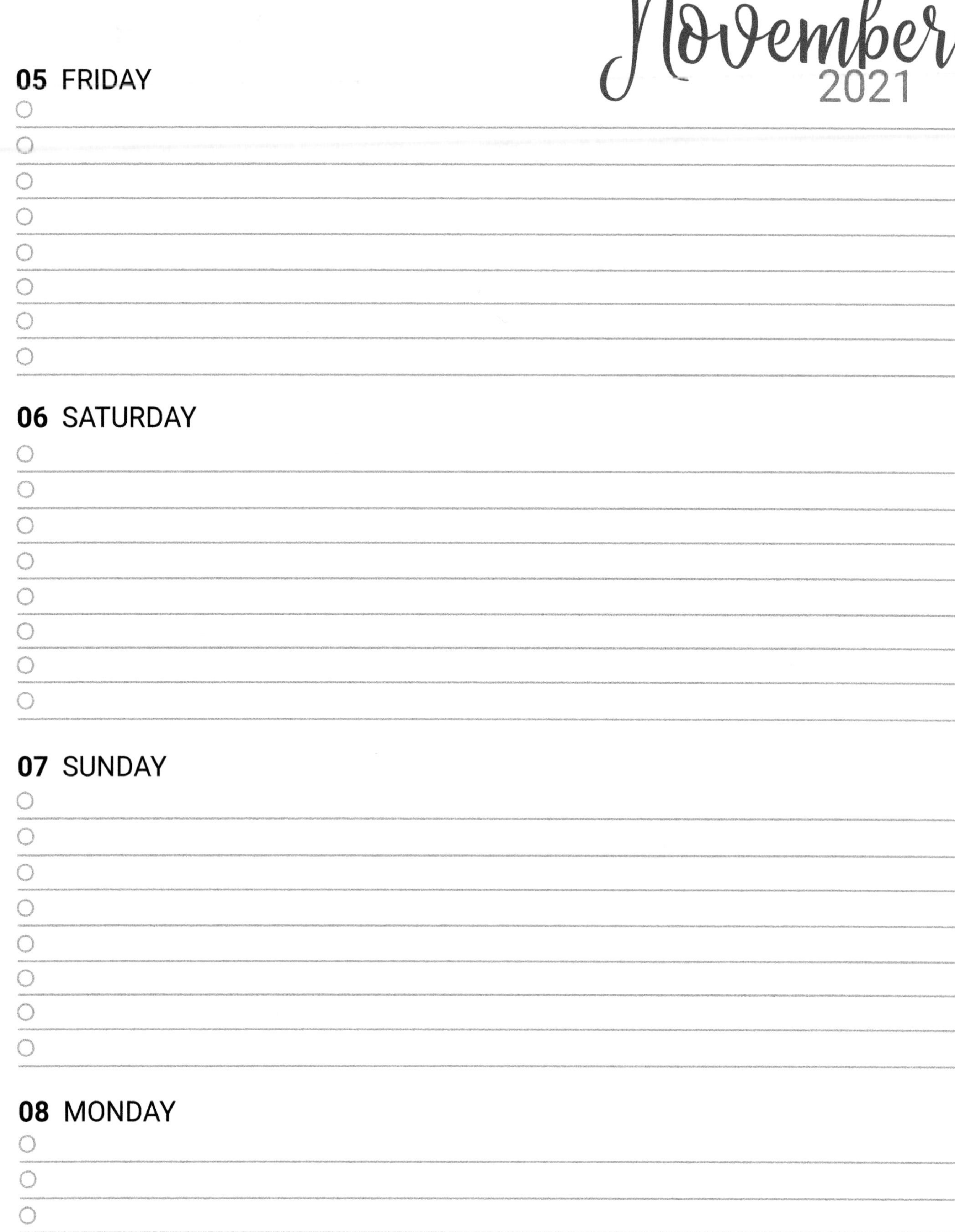

05 FRIDAY

06 SATURDAY

07 SUNDAY

08 MONDAY

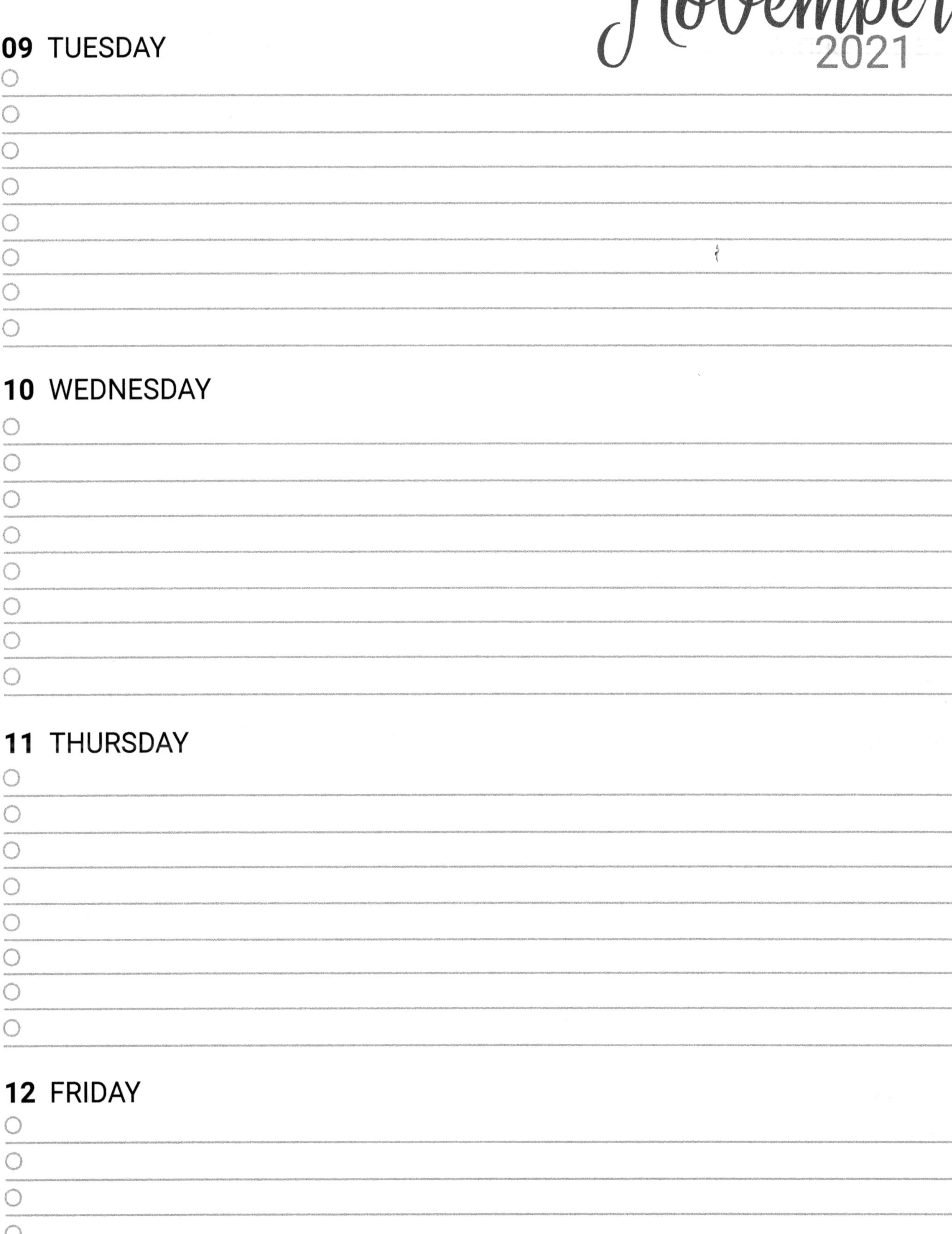

November
2021

09 TUESDAY

10 WEDNESDAY

11 THURSDAY

12 FRIDAY

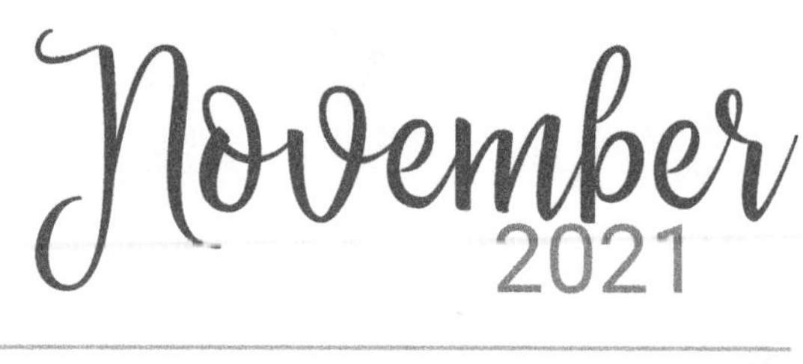

13 SATURDAY

14 SUNDAY

15 MONDAY

16 TUESDAY

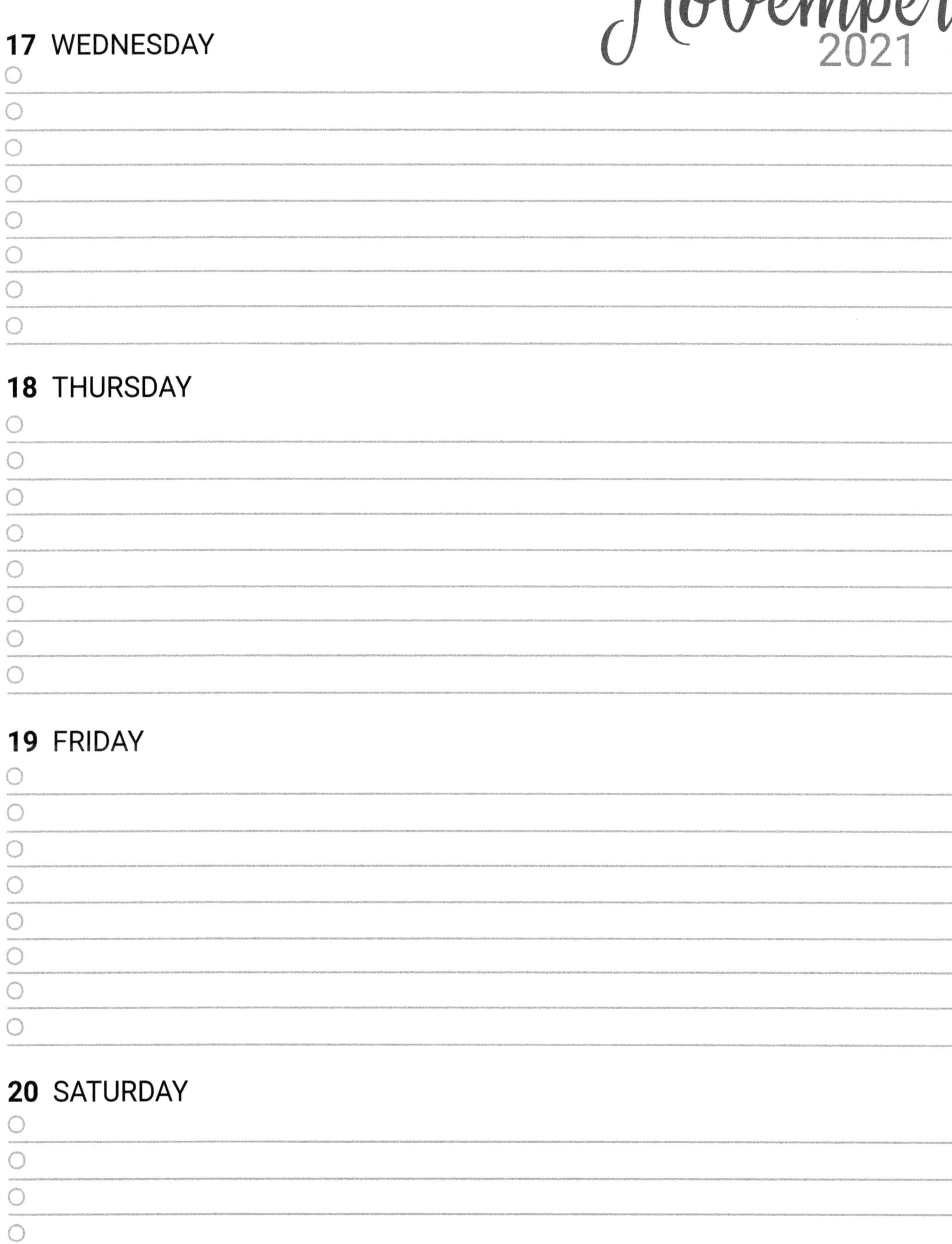

17 WEDNESDAY

18 THURSDAY

19 FRIDAY

20 SATURDAY

November
2021

21 SUNDAY

22 MONDAY

23 TUESDAY

24 WEDNESDAY

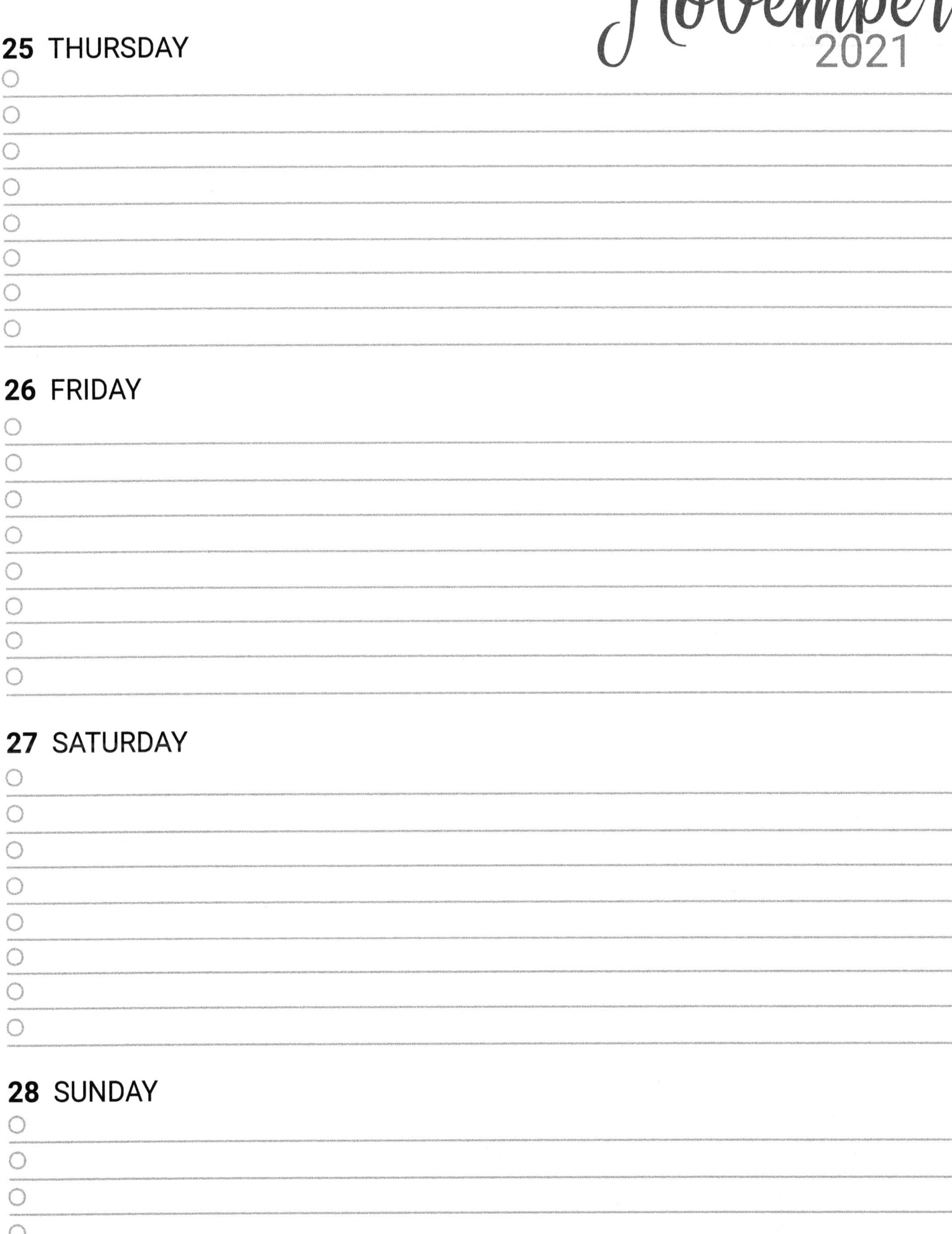

25 THURSDAY

26 FRIDAY

27 SATURDAY

28 SUNDAY

29 MONDAY

30 TUESDAY

NOTES

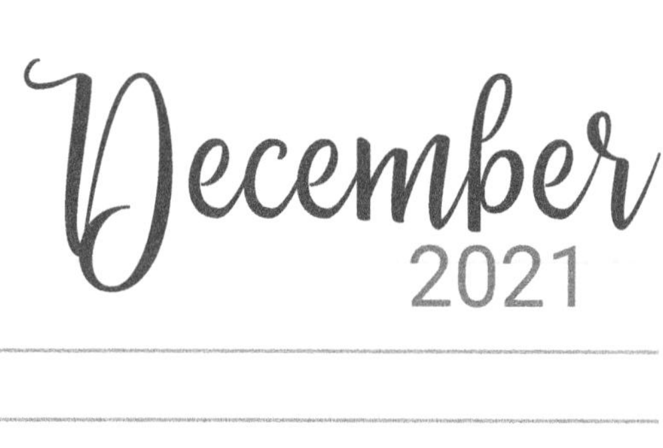

01 WEDNESDAY

02 THURSDAY

03 FRIDAY

04 SATURDAY

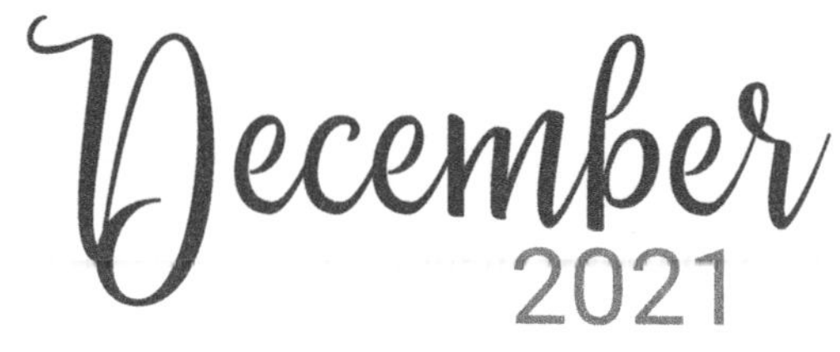

December
2021

05 SUNDAY

06 MONDAY

07 TUESDAY

08 WEDNESDAY

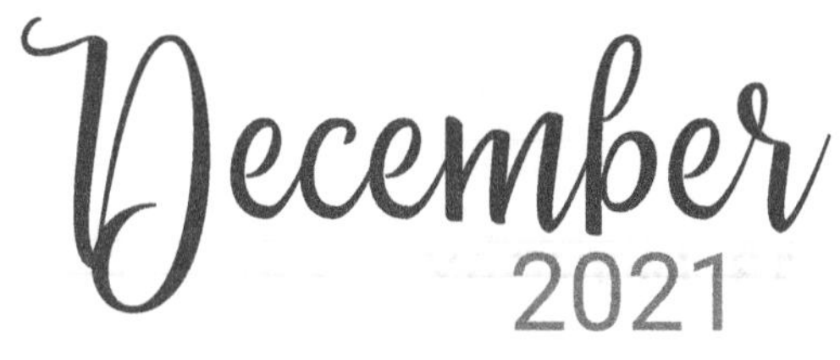

09 THURSDAY

10 FRIDAY

11 SATURDAY

12 SUNDAY

13 MONDAY

14 TUESDAY

15 WEDNESDAY

16 THURSDAY

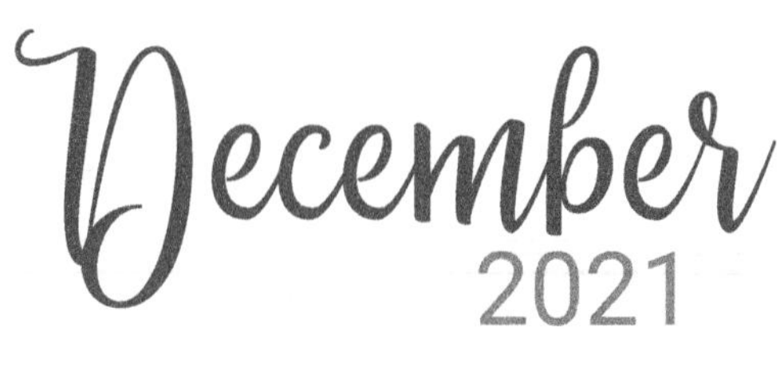

17 FRIDAY

○
○
○
○
○
○
○
○

18 SATURDAY

○
○
○
○
○
○
○
○

19 SUNDAY

○
○
○
○
○
○
○
○

20 MONDAY

○
○
○
○
○

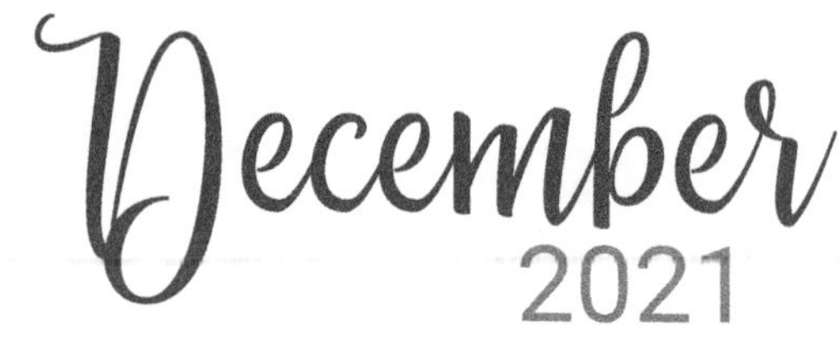

21 TUESDAY

22 WEDNESDAY

23 THURSDAY

24 FRIDAY

25 SATURDAY

26 SUNDAY

27 MONDAY

28 TUESDAY

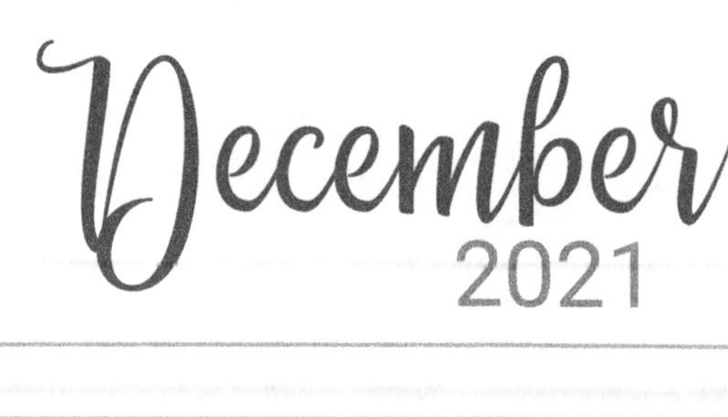

December
2021

29 WEDNESDAY

30 THURSDAY

31 FRIDAY

NOTES

CPSIA information can be obtained
at www.ICGtesting.com
Printed in the USA
BVHW051556090921
616447BV00013B/379

9 781970 177336